God's Positioning System

God's Positioning System

Tonia Strong

Columbus, Ohio

The views and opinions expressed in this book are solely those of the author and do not reflect the views or opinions of Gatekeeper Press. Gatekeeper Press is not to be held responsible for and expressly disclaims responsibility of the content herein.

God's Positioning System

Published by Gatekeeper Press
2167 Stringtown Rd, Suite 109
Columbus, OH 43123-2989
www.GatekeeperPress.com

Copyright © 2022 by Tonia Strong
All rights reserved. Neither this book, nor any parts within it may be sold or reproduced in any form or by any electronic or mechanical means, including information storage and retrieval systems, without permission in writing from the author. The only exception is by a reviewer, who may quote short excerpts in a review.

Library of Congress Control Number: 2021950001

ISBN (paperback): 9781662920776
eISBN: 9781662920783

Truck driving. Truck driving on a clear, sun-filled day. Normal traffic flow, not too fast, not too slow. Going to someplace on the other side of DFW. Yep, I get paid to road-trip.

Being a driver was not my life dream. The original plan was to be like my dad, a truck mechanic. But I wanted to be able to empathize with a customer about the issues they needed fixed. I didn't like the thought of someone fixing a truck without ever having the pleasure of really being reliant on it working properly.

Joining the military got me the needed experience to know how to be a mechanic—you know, the basics of finding the problem—but it didn't give me true experience at fixing anything. The military taught me how to be a changer of parts, not a mechanic that repairs parts. This may have been different if I'd served during wartime, but I was in the post-Iraq War tedium period of the Army. I was taught if it doesn't work, just replace it. It wasn't our job to "fix;" it was our job to keep the vehicle running now. Just take the bad part out, put a good part in, and move on to the next vehicle.

After being honorably discharged from the military, I needed to learn to drive a truck and live in it to appreciate not only the job but the vehicle itself. I attended truck driving school and worked as a driver. I fell in love with driving. I wanted to get away from people, and this was a perfect career for someone who, at best, tolerated the general public.

Driving has been my career since 1996. I've gotten stuck in the mud in Ohio, shut down from a blizzard in South Dakota, in a staring competition with a moose in Maine, trapped on the GW Bridge in New York for eight hours, and watched a bighorn sheep ram a stopped Mercedes in Colorado. I've seen a few things in this career. What I don't like is fog. Before the age of GPS, fog was my worst weather condition for driving. It was kind of tolerable while staying on the interstate, but if you had to get off and look for street signs, low bridge warning signs, truck-restricted route signs, or addresses to businesses, it sucked!

Now, it's not too bad. With a global positioning system, you can get such an accurate location that it's almost gospel to automatically turn on the street the unit tells you to turn on. It's wrong so rarely that you just take it for granted. When you put the address in and look at the overall route, it seems fine. So you put the truck in gear and get paid to go on that road trip. Of course, you still have to be mindful of vehicles on shoulders, animals that may attempt to cross the road, or even stopped traffic that is practically invisible until you're right there.

But how do you know when you're following God's positioning system? Where's the lavender line to tell you which decision to make, or if you should even be on the road at all? Just like the GPS on the dash, zooming out lets you get a big picture of things, and zooming in puts the finer points on the route you're traveling. And so it is in our lives as well.

Calculating route... 12%
October 1982

"Let's go to my house and play?" She always wanted to go to her house to play, never just stay there at the playground. My mom never agreed, so going through the motions of asking her seemed like a waste of time. "Please? It's really cool at my house. Go ask, please?" she would say, begging.

"Okay," I said. If playing this out would get her to focus on our current game, what was the harm?

We went around the corner to my house, and I went inside. Mom wasn't feeling well that day, but that seemed to happen more often than not lately. She was propped up in bed with the pillows behind her back, watching some soap opera.

"Can I go to Laurie's house and play?" I asked.

"Be back before the lights come on," she said.

What? Cool, this will be a new adventure! "Yes, ma'am!" I ran outside and told Laurie, and we were off. We went back past the playground and planned our new game. We were still going to play hide-and-seek, but now we could only play in the house. Since both of us would usually be outside, playing in the house was going to be a challenge. We determined that the only room off-limits was the bathroom. There was really no place to hide in a bathroom anyway, so the rule sounded good to me.

Getting to her house, we went inside, and her brother was there. She explained that we were going to play hide-and-seek.

"Can I play too?"

He's like fifteen. Why would he want to play hide-and-seek with a couple of seven-year-olds? I thought.

"Okay," Laurie said, with all the enthusiasm of a death-row inmate.

"You start counting, Laurie," he replied, "and Tonia and I will hide." He got up from the couch and ushered me down a hallway toward the bedrooms. I could hear Laurie counting, and I was thinking of how easy a closet would be to get caught in. *Need a better hiding place than that.* My next thought was under the bed, but I didn't know how clean they kept their house. *What if it's dirty? Don't want to go home filthy either.*

He pulled me into a bedroom with a big TV sitting on the dresser. In my house, the only rooms with TVs were the living room and my parents' bedroom.

"Is this your room?" I asked.

"Yep. You like it?"

"Sure." Looking around and going with a sure loser of a hiding place, I headed toward the closet.

"You don't have to hide just yet. She's still counting." I stopped and looked at him. "Sit here. Let's talk."

Wondering why he wanted to talk, I sat next to him on the bed. I looked down at the floor and noticed dust bunnies. *Good thing I didn't choose under the bed.*

"So, you ever kissed a boy?"

Recalculating... 17%
August 1983

This isn't supposed to happen this way, I don't think. Moms aren't supposed to die before their moms, are they? Mom's mom is still alive, so this is wrong, out of order.

My dad sat me on the curb outside our little house and told me my mom was dead. At eight years old, I knew she wasn't coming back in my rational mind, but hearing him say those words made it seem impossible. Dead? My mom? The word for that moment is called 'surreal,' but at the time I just thought this would change any minute now. *This moment isn't really happening, and I'll wake up soon. Just hold on. I'm supposed to have a mom.*

All of my extended family, both Mom's side and Dad's, lived in Michigan; and being that my dad wasn't planning on raising a child alone, we moved. New Mexico to Michigan is quite the culture shock, not to mention the weather difference. At first, we lived with his mom, and I started attending Alexander Elementary School, which was literally across the street from Grandma's back door.

Acquiring Satellites... 32%
Zoom In

Grandma's house is old and creaky. Weird sounds I'm not used to at night, and the smell of old person is everywhere. This is the first time I've been in a two-story house. There are three bedrooms upstairs, two bedrooms and two bathrooms downstairs, and the bathroom directly at the bottom of the stairs is considered the one for "all us young 'uns." My room is directly across from the top step of the stairs. My dad's room is downstairs, next to Grandma's.

Our house in New Mexico was three bedrooms, and I slept on a futon in my parents' room. My sisters had to share one bedroom and my brother had the other. But now I have the entire upstairs to myself like a little kingdom. I go from room to room, playing my imaginary games and fighting off imaginary dragons.

Since my dad's siblings haven't seen him in quite some time, it's like a sleepover almost every weekend. An aunt from Illinois came with her kids to visit for a few days, and I had to pick a room to be mine while they were here. I picked the smallest room because it had a cool little window seat in it. You can look out and see so many lights that it always sparks my imaginings of far-off lands, with heros and villians to conquer.

I have my favorite pj's in the biggest room, the one my cousin is sleeping in. It has a huge closet, bigger than any I've ever seen before. Not only can I walk in it, I can make a whole other room out of it! At bedtime, I ask if I can get them. "Sure," he says. "Don't forget to turn the lights off before you change."

"Why?" I ask.

"Look." He points out the window. "From the outside, if the lights are on, people can see in."

"Oh, okay." I've never thought about that. He walks out and closes the door behind him.

I'm undressed, about to get my pj pants on, when he comes back into the room, looking over his shoulder. The lighs are off and I can't see his face, but I get the impression something's wrong. He rushes over to me and pulls me into the closet, pushing me roughly onto the floor where I fall facedown.

"What's going on?" I yell. "What are you doing?"

Wrapping one hand over my mouth, he uses his other to take his pants down. I freeze, in my mind and physically. All I hear is my own heartbeat in my ears. I think this is going to be like

Laurie's brother, but it's not. Laying his entire body on top of mine from behind, he pushes himself into the wrong place. It hurts. A lot. My tears running down my cheeks make his grip slippery on my face, which causes him to squeeze harder around my jaw. That just makes me cry more.

He never says a word. When he's finished, he pushes himself up by placing his hands on my back for leverage, as if trying to push me into the floorboards. I hear him zip his pants up. The door opens and closes but I don't open my eyes. I think *he's left the room* but after a beat, he half-drags, half-prods me up and across the landing into the smaller room I was going to sleep in. Drops me on the floor next to the bed then goes back and gets my PJs. Throws them on the floor next to me, then he's gone. I have to crawl to the door to close it because he didn't. He couldn't even grant me that measure of humanity.

In the morning, an eon later, the bed is full of blood. I throw away my PJs and hide the sheets. I stain a pair of pants sitting in church, and Grandma remarks that I'm young to be starting my period. He is standing right there so I know not to say anything, Laurie's brother taught me that much.

If this is what it means to be a girl, I don't want to be one.

Zoom Out

We didn't stay with her long, and eventually we got a place down the street, which meant I could stay in the same school. My dad thought I needed a mentor, so he enrolled me in the Big Brothers/Big Sisters program, and I met the woman who would become my Big Sister. She had never married and had a condition called endometriosis, which made her unable to have children of her own. She had two sisters and a brother who had parented good-sized families. I'm sure by the time she was a mentor to me, she had assumed she'd never become a parent.

She listened to classical music and NPR whenever the radio was on. On the TV was the evening news and *Star Trek: The Next Generation.* She worked at an art museum, so I always got to see the new exhibits when they came. I got to stay with her sometimes while she worked, and I would run the "back-up" tapes for the accounting department. She was vastly different from anyone in my family, and I never had a bad time with her.

When my dad asked me if I wanted to return to New Mexico, I said, "Yes." As much as I liked my Big Sister, it wasn't 75 degrees in January like New Mexico. We moved back, and I went to the school I would've attended if we hadn't moved in the first place—Kennedy Middle School.

Dad tried to put me in the program again, but it wasn't such a smooth transition this time. I didn't like them. They were never as cool as the original Big Sister, and I made sure they knew it. After going through three, their agency called Michigan's and asked for help. The OG Big Sister called me and said to give them a chance; I might learn something new. Fine! #4 was the longest one I stayed with until I was removed from my dad's custody.

Oh, have I not mentioned Dad was a raging alcoholic?

Zoom In

Dad puts something that looks like water to my nine-year-old eyes into his coffee. He just bought the little bottle with the white label and red lettering from the store, but he always waits until he's in the car to put it in the coffee. He never lets me drink the stuff either, says it's not for kids. I have to admit, it smells funny, like the stuff Mom used to put on my cuts when I'd fall. I think it's alcohol.

Zoom Out

Before we left Michigan, we'd developed a system. If the phone rang on a Friday or Saturday night and he wasn't home, let it ring.

One ring and then silence meant he'd been arrested and wouldn't be home until Monday after school or sometime on Tuesday. He explained, "When you're arrested, you get one call. If someone answers the phone, no more calls for the person dialing. If no one answers, then the person can call someone else to try and make bail. So after you, I'll use my next attempt on the bail bondsman so I can get out sooner."

This was when the rough times started. The state of New Mexico removed me from my dad's custody, and a sister offered to take me in. Sounds like a good enough move, right? Not so much. I love my sister, don't get me wrong, but we didn't grow up together. She's 20 years older than me, and we had nothing in common. She has two children older than me! And guess what? She's back in Michigan!

I stayed with her for a while, and we learned that I was already a grown-up at the age of 11. I did my own laundry, made my own meals, got up and went to school wearing what I wanted to wear, and no, that did not include dresses. I do not like hanging out with other people, and I'm not a social butterfly. She stuck it out for 18 months, then declared I had to go.

A cousin took me in, and I went downhill even faster. With my sister, I was getting good grades and going to school, but with the cousin, not so much. The only good thing was, I was back in the same city with my Big Sister, and she kept me from freefalling off the deep end.

Then she got an idea. What if I moved in with her? Well, I'd tried the family situation, and that wasn't working, so why not? She moved me in halfway through my sophomore year in high school. I had a new mom.

Zoom In
Summer 1988

I hate video games. I've never been good at the mental speed needed for winning at them. A doctor told me once that the condition is called 'psychomotor retardation' and results from one or both parents being alcoholics at conception. My nephew doesn't have that problem and loves playing in front of a screen. I've always admired the time and effort needed to master anything, but have never had the inclination to put forth the effort on a video game.

While watching him, I got bored. We were downstairs in the basement of my sister's house. Well, it was my house too, since I'd moved in after leaving my dad. There was an old couch, a recliner, and a glass coffee table. The old big-screen TV from upstairs had been demoted to our TV in the basement.

My room was also down there. It was behind the window blinds used to separate it from the rest of the basement. My nephew is three years older than me, and we bring our boyfriends and girlfriends down there to hang out and watch TV or listen to music or other things. Being only eleven, I'm not supposed to be doing any of that stuff, but I do it anyway.

My sister called me from upstairs. "Coming," I responded. I hadn't been living with her very long, and it still felt like I was on some kind of extended vacation. In other words, I was still being polite like a good girl should.

When you come up the stairs, you have to make a sharp left, or you'll walk out the side door of the house. Turning left, you're in the open-air dining room/living room but looking into the kitchen. She was sitting on the couch in the living room folding laundry, and I sat at the dining-room table, putting the table and most of the room between us.

"So, tell me what's been going on with you and your dad that you have to come here? Is he drinking more than he used to?" she asked.

"No." I blamed myself for telling the Big Sister in New Mexico that I didn't want to be with him anymore. I was only looking for attention and, like any good busybody, she swooped right in to help. "He's drinking about the same as always, I guess."

"Did he ever do anything to you?"

"Like what?" I asked apprehensively.

"Touch you or molest you?"

"No," I replied, looking down at my reflection in the glass of the table.

"Did any of his friends?"

"Dad doesn't have any friends."

Should I tell her? Trying to distract myself by listening to the sounds of the video game being played downstairs, I mulled over telling her about Laurie's brother all those years ago or my cousin shortly after we'd moved in with Grandma. *Does it even matter anymore? I've never told anyone, like they said. No one.*

"Has anyone ever done anything to you?" she asked, but she was not looking at me. I could see her reflection in the glass of the table as well, and she was looking at the laundry.

I decided to tell her. I thought she cared. I mean, she's family, and since family is always supposed to take care of each other, she had to, right? For example, Mom's brother moved his whole family to New Mexico for a while before she died. They lived across the street from us, like family is supposed to.

"I was molested by a friend's brother when I was seven," I mumbled.

"I can't hear you," she said.

Repeating my answer, I noticed that the video game music had stopped and that my nephew was listening. We always snooped on each other getting in trouble. But, since I didn't do anything wrong here, he was going to be disappointed. The thought brought a smile to my mind.

"How could you let that happen?"

How could I...? Oh, okay. Apparently, I did do something wrong. He said that Mom would get in trouble if I didn't do what he said, or told anyone what was going on. It happened so often over the course of that year, and Mom was so sick, I didn't want to bring her bad news when she was feeling well. I didn't want to make things harder for her. And now, having confirmation that I had done something wrong, I would not tell about him or anyone else again.

Mom died not knowing.

Zoom In

August 1991

In the car going to see my dad. He's in a hospital north of Chicago. Someone got in touch with Mom's foster parent agency and said he's in bad shape, that he was asking for me.

We get there and he's hooked up to all kinds of tubes and hoses. IV here, oxygen there, feeding tube here, colostomy bag there. His skin is grey, and he's lost a lot of weight since the last time I'd seen him some months ago.

"I didn't do it," he moans. He's pulling the feeding tube out of his mouth, but he doesn't look like he's awake.

"You've got to keep an eye on him about this," the doctor explains. "He keeps pulling it out because it's uncomfortable, but it's the only way he can eat. He's had about two feet of bowel removed and is battling an infection. He'd been sick a long time before he came here." The doctor looks at me like he wants to say more, but stops. He looks at Mom and says, "We're just trying to make him as comfortable as possible right now."

"I'll leave you alone with him for a while, Tonia," she says as they both step quietly out of the room.

"Dad?" I whisper. "I'm here."

"I didn't do it," he mumbles around the tube.

"Didn't do what?" I ask.

My dad's sister suddenly walks in the room. "Hi, Tonia," she says. "It's been so long since I've seen you!" I can't recall that I've ever met her, but she seems to think I remember her. "How are you?"

"I'm fine," I answer.

"You might not know this, but your dad was in some trouble a while ago." She sits in the chair against the wall facing the bed. "He was arrested and charged with raping a white girl in Mississippi. So, if you hear him mumbling, it might be related to that." I remember seeing a picture in the newspaper about him being exonerated for some crime, but didn't know the details.

Then he walks in; her son. I do remember him. This cousin of mine who pulled me into the walk-in closet upstairs in my grandma's house when I was nine and raped me. "I need to see my mom," I say to escape the hug he is attempting to put on me. *Why are all these people here? They never cared for my dad or me! F*ck them!*

I smoke a few cigarettes in the courtyard of the hospital. Eventually, I go back up and I sit with my dad alone. Mom and I stay in a hotel not too far away and return to Dad over the course of the weekend. On Sunday, I tell him I have to go back home so I can go to school in the morning, and that I love him. The whole weekend, he never seems to be there anyway, but it still hurts to leave him.

Mom tells me on Monday morning that he died overnight.

Acquiring Satelites...57%

Zoom Out

Getting used to going to church every Sunday with my new mom was easy at first. I loved learning new things, and even though my birth mom took me when I was younger, I don't really remember it well. I have a vague recollection of getting baptized because my friend didn't want to do it alone, but other than that, nothing really. But this mom, the one who God shoehorned into my life, goes every Sunday. I'd have to get an excused letter signed by at least two presidents to get out of it.

I learned a little about God during service, but most of the education was in rituals:

- Don't make change out of the collection money
- Don't sit too close to the preacher because you won't be able to hide when you get sleepy
- Do sit close to the speakers to hide your voice when pretending to sing
- Learn the songs, it's easier than trying to read the fine print in the hymnal
- Get a bible cover but keep it closed so no one knows how often you don't read it
- Put book tabs on it so if you do have to open the cover you can find Haggai like you know where it is

You know, stuff like that...

I had a hard time reconciling the God of love and mercy with the God who told the Israelites to kill all the people in Canaan. The same God who people at the church say knows what's going to happen before it does, and yet didn't stop the abuse and assaults I went through.

Recalculating... 41%
Summer 1992

I had a car and no place to go. *How about the cousins on Lafayette Street?* I thought. *That's always interesting. We'll see what's going on.*

Driving from the 'burbs in Wyoming to Grand Rapids was the only interesting part of that day. Getting to the house and seeing no one home, I moved on to find an aunt to visit, knowing I'd get the proverbial "you look so much like your mother" but willing to endure it to get to know my mom better. Recently coming to the realization that I didn't remember what she looked like anymore hurt me a lot. Like I betrayed her in some way. So now I'm trying to learn about her through those who knew her.

I got to my aunt's house and rang the bell. Cousin answered. "Hey! She's not home but you can hang with me if you want. Just down here watching TV."

Trying to hide my disappointment, I said, "Sure. What's on?"

"Hell if I know. I'm just smoking a little and staring." He led me down the stairs to the basement and sat in the middle of the couch. I was forced to pick a side; I chose, then sat too.

"Ah, Maury." *The Maury Povich Show*, the epitome of stupid people showing off their stupidity. We watched in silence for a while, then I asked, "Is she coming home soon?"

"I don't know." He held out the bowl he'd been smoking marijuana from. "You want some?"

"Sure." I needed something to relax me. I get nervous around guys. *I shouldn't feel this way around a cousin, just calm down.* He handed me the bowl and I smoked a little, then coughed a little.

I moved to return the bowl to him; he grabbed my arm and pinned me to the couch. I tried to fight but it was pointless. Placing his hand over my mouth, he whispered, "Let's just have some fun and keep this quiet." He turned me over and pulled my shorts down. I didn't scream or cry. I must attract this.

Recalculating... 21%

The itching won't stop! I've tried every yeast infection treatment out there. What's going on? What's that in the bed? Looking closely, it looks like a tiny crab. No way. I told my mom I had headlice, and she bought some stuff at the store. She didn't know why there'd be a headlice infestation going on at a high school without her getting some kind of notice, but that's what I told her, and she didn't argue.

Acquiring Satellites...34%
Autumn 1993

After I graduated high school, I put in the requisite college application and waited anxiously for a letter of acceptance to arrive. I applied to one school. I'd visited Michigan State and didn't enjoy the experience, and the University of Michigan was too far away for my comfort. But almost across the street was a pretty good private school which happened to be Christian as well.

As a graduation present, my mom had taken me on a cruise to see the Virgin Islands. I had insisted on being baptized before I went but nothing seemed to happen spiritually. I guess I thought things would miraculously feel different, being "filled with the Holy Spirit" and all, but nope. Now my thinking was, *If I get in to this school, God will surely show Himself to me in a way that can't be mistaken for coincidence.*

I'm not sure how much I believed in a Christian God at this point in my life. I think I was testing Him to see what He'd do. I did remember Him stating, "You shall have no other Gods before me" (Genesis 20:3), but what exactly does that mean? I hear all the time that we're all worshipping the same God, but that in different cultures He takes on different forms. Makes sense, but some of those other cultures aren't nice to Christians or Jews, so are we really? Christians haven't always been sweethearts, but is it all the same? Basically, we hate each other religiously. *That doesn't sound right.*

So when I got that acceptance letter from this school, I thought I'd really be learning from believers living a believer's life, in a Christ-filled setting with others truly seeking a greater understanding of what and who we believed in! It took about three weeks for me to see that they're just as screwed up as the rest of us. I wasn't going to get answers to my questions here. Especially questions I didn't know how to ask. I went through my days searching for something I didn't know how to find, or know what it would look like even if I found it. I decided to try out a new place.

Back in the day, before there was Facebook or Twitter, there were chatrooms. In the basement of my dorm was a lab with plenty of computers to get into all kinds of trouble. Someone was caught downloading inappropriate photos to save to their floppy disk. Even the name of the device sounds gross.

I'd get bored and head there to find a chatroom to talk to people. As much as I don't like talking to people face-to-face, chatrooms were a great middle ground for someone with social anxiety disorder, i.e. me. I met someone there, and we started talking about religion. I explained that I was a student at a Christian college in the US, and they said they were at work in Pakistan. I thought, *How cool is this? Meeting someone from halfway around the world!*

We talked about their religion of Islam, and I wanted to know more. I don't really know what possessed me to ask about it, but they were more than willing to send some books and guide me through my conversion. *Wait, what? I'll take the books so I can learn for myself, but I don't think I'll be converting anytime soon.*

The books arrived—a Quran and some other books that I don't remember now—and I started reading. I continued to talk to this person in the chatroom from time to time, but school was starting to interfere with my social time. Who would've thought that college schoolwork could be time-consuming?

After a few days of lackluster "studying" of these Islam books, I lost my patience and just asked my chatroom friend, "How do I convert?" They told me that I just had to face the east and pray to Allah, and it was done. No one had to witness it or anything.

Hmmm, sure, what else do I got going on…? I got a prayer rug and started praying five times a day, facing the east and reading as much of these books as I could.

Then the insomnia started. It wasn't too bad at first. A couple of nights a week, I'd toss and turn seemingly all night long. I was starting to drive my roommate insane. She didn't really care about any of the weird stuff I was getting into, except when it kept her awake at night. It was getting difficult to get up and go to class in the morning, even though my first class wasn't until 9 AM.

I would pray to Allah to help with the lack of sleep and my inability to pay attention in class. Thinking that my insomnia was causing the poor attention problems, I kept praying and hoping things would change. They got worse.

I was working on campus as a dispatcher for the school's police department. I went to bed around 5 or 6 PM until the alarm woke me up at 11 PM, punched in at the station by 11:30 PM, and punched out around 8 AM. I basically monitored the fire alarms on campus, where I might occasionally get a disturbance call. It was a Christian school, not exactly a hotbed of crime; but it was my job, and I wanted to do it as well as possible.

I started seeing movement in the corners of my eyes at random moments. Just the tail end of shapes or shadows, but when I looked there'd be nothing there. Roomie was going home for Thanksgiving, but I was staying. I still couldn't get any sleep, but I was almost starting to get used to it. She was leaving on Wednesday, and I'd be "home alone" until Sunday afternoon. I was working the entire weekend, so maybe I could catch up on schoolwork and sleep without her creeping around the room in the afternoon, trying to be quiet for my benefit but not pulling it off very well.

The first night, Wednesday, went off without a hitch. I slept well, even though I had to listen to the entrance door to the dorm opening and closing nonstop most of the afternoon and evening while everyone was leaving. I got up and went to work that night. Nothing of note happened. I got back to my room in the morning and sat at the desk to get some work done. There it was again, that shadow! It had to be because I was tired. At one time, I might have heard a sound move along with the shadow, but I wasn't really sure, so I dismissed it. I decided I was going to pray to Allah more fervently than before, so he could help me get back on track. My prayers were getting desperate, since the lack of sleep was really starting to build up.

After dinner, I lay down for bed when the phone rang. *Who the hell is calling?* I picked up the phone and answered—nothing. *Great, thanks!* I went back to bed. The phone rang again. *You're kidding, right?* I jumped up to answer—again, nothing. Not even heavy breathing. *I NEED SLEEP!* I unplugged the phone; that'd fix it. The rest of the weekend was a battle of paranoid thoughts. Was I going crazy, or was there something to be worried about? But the increase in shadowy figures flinting out of my range of vision, and drastic changes in room temperature, were noticed by others and not just me.

The phone ringing and no one being on the line got old the first time it happened; now, it was expected. The calls seemed to only happen when I had to go to work, of course. I needed to get my sleep, or I was pretty much useless, not just for work but for class as well, so the phone waking me up was a big deal. Sometimes we'd just unplug it from the wall except when Roomie was waiting for a call. (No one had a cell phone back in those days—landline only. You were hot stuff if you had a pager.)

Not only were there incessant calls, but for weeks the room had been getting darker somehow. I don't know how to explain it, but it was duller. More than the seasons changing and the night starting sooner—it was dingier. The colors in the room couldn't get bright, no matter what we did. Roomie noticed too but thought it was just because we were no longer new students; we were used to seeing them now. But I seemed to notice the colors being dimmer all over campus, not just our room. *Couldn't have anything to do with those books, could it?* I spent the entire Thanksgiving break praying for relief from the ever-pervasive darkness that seemed to be taking over me and everything I looked at.

Between Thanksgiving and Christmas break, everything escalated slowly. The phone ringing and no one being on the line was even getting to Roomie. Me not sleeping was a big deal. Obviously, I managed to get some kind of sleep, or I'd have truly started hallucinating. During the day, in class or at work, I was fine, but at home the shadowy shapes I'd see floating around the room were very creepy, and I really wanted them to disappear. I was praying and facing the east and doing everything these books said I should do, but nothing was making this better.

Christmas break started on a Tuesday, and once again I'd be staying on campus to work. Roomie and all the other girls in my pod were going home. The building was going to be quieter than it was during Thanksgiving! However, since I wouldn't be doing schoolwork (finals were done), all I had to do was watch TV and sleep when not at work. Fantastic!

It really ratcheted up the first night. The phone started. I didn't even wait, and immediately I unplugged it. I didn't have to work that night, but no one was calling me anyway. The faucet in the bathroom turned on. Being that I wasn't used to that sound, it took me a few minutes to realize what it was. I went in and shut it off, returning to *Rudolf, The Red-Nosed Reindeer*. A couple of minutes later, it was on again. Shadow—over there. No, there was nothing there.

Show's over anyway. I'm going to bed. I turned on the lights to use the bathroom. After washing my hands, I reached to turn the lights off, and the switch was ice cold. In the darkness, I felt something slide along the back of my legs. *WTF!* I hit the switch again, and the shadows were almost EVERYWHERE around me! I blinked; they were gone. *What is happening to me? I am going insane.* I made it to the bed, still seeing the shadows in the corner of my eye, but nothing was there. I got in bed and tried to sleep. It took some time, but it did happen.

I must admit that I'd lost my want of Allah by this point. I was not sleeping. I was seeing shadowy figures that looked kind of like the remnants of cigarette smoke almost everywhere I looked: in my room, at work, walking around campus—everywhere. I was scared. I was ashamed of walking away from the Jesus I'd spent my life believing in, and I didn't think He wanted me back. He'd have spared me from all of this if He wanted me, right?

This had to be part of my depression. Sleep deprivation is no joke. People can go crazy from it. But is that what was happening? I did want sleep, but I couldn't get it. I'd tried all sorts of over-the-counter medications; even old faithful, NyQuil, did absolutely nothing. I had to fix this somehow. *Maybe I need to see a therapist again.*

The rest of the week was a continuation of everything that had already been happening. No sleep. If I plugged in the phone, it would ring with no one on the other end. The faucet in the bathroom kept turning on. And the shadows...oh, the shadows were the worst. I could hear them now. Not speech or anything, just the sound of wind when you open the car windows going down the road, just a bee flying next to your ear, just cloth rubbing against itself like the sound of a nylon windbreaker being worn. Just all of that for a week!

Sleep was a stranger to me. I was tossing and turning, trying to figure out why I was having these issues. I had never had this kind of weirdness happen before. The phone rang. *NO!! Not tonight!* I jumped out of bed and got to the phone, just to realize it was already unplugged from the previous night's adventure. I stared, confused. *What's going on?! Why is it so dark in here all the time now?*

Crawling back into bed, I faced the wall and asked the empty air to help me sleep. Pulling the blankets up to my neck, I noticed how incredibly cold it was in the room. Eyes closed, I heard fabric being rubbed together from the direction of the door into the room. Turning over, I looked—of course, nothing was there. Those shadows were swarming now. As I started to return to my wall-facing position, I saw these two shapes on my roommate's bed. They looked like clouds of smoke. Separate and distinct, I felt like they were looking at me. They didn't have any form to them, just smoke that wasn't dissipating.

I slowly turned away from the forms on the other bed to face the wall again, thinking this was all in my head. *HOLY SH*T!!!!!!!* The black-and-white Janet Jackson poster at the foot of my bed had red cat-like eyes looking at me! The red eyes weren't where her eyes would be; instead, they appeared to be coming out of her cheeks. "Oh, f*ck," I whispered. I was frozen. Then the eyes moved toward me from the wall. Smoke appeared to be coming from the poster—smoke that was congealing into the shape of an arm but no hand. The end of the arm closest to me wrapped itself around my ankle, and I felt pressure. *It's real! It's pulling me!* Scared and barely breathing, I could feel my heart pounding out of my chest.

I tried to think. *What do I do? How do I stop this? What exactly is this, anyway?*

You know what this is. Don't try to act innocent now. This is Evil with a capital E!

Where's my Bible?

On the bookshelf behind you.

I reached behind my head to the top of my bookshelf without glancing away from the red eyes. It was right there. I grabbed it and pulled it to my chest, whispering, "Save me!" The tears were making things blurry, and I'd lost track of the two things that were on my roommate's bed. But I suddenly didn't care. I felt like lying down, so I did. Lying back on the bed and holding the Bible to my chest, I fell asleep.

Ten hours later, I opened my eyes, lying in the same position I had fallen asleep. Looking at the boring Janet Jackson poster I'd had on my wall for years, I now saw no red eyes, no smoky arms reaching out to touch me, no nothing! I felt completely refreshed, and the room looked brighter somehow.

I wasn't sure what had happened those last months, but I was guessing it was supernatural. I thanked God for saving me from whatever would have happened if I hadn't grabbed my Bible. But that was about all I did. I didn't share the experience with anyone, assuming they'd think me nuts for seeing demons and shadowy figures everywhere I looked. After my return, if you will, to Christianity, I kept the entire incident to myself. I didn't even tell my roommate when she commented on how brighter the room looked after the Christmas break. Filed away, not to be thought or spoken of in public.

Recalculating...6%
Spring 1994

I met her at a bar. I didn't know I was a classmate until she told me we had Spanish 101 together. Here's a girl going to the same school I was going to and she says she's Christian and the old men that wrote the Bible didn't want anyone different so they made up the whole "homosexuality is a sin" thing.

Once you've been tramatized by fire, you're very conscious of everything even remotely colored orange or yellow emanating heat. But this was a blue flame. Maybe this is where I should go? Maybe I can find someplace where I feel comfortable in my own skin. After the things that have happened, I feel awkward when friends want to talk about boys, I don't care about them and I don't want to talk about them. My guy friends never talk about girls around me so I don't feel weird. I don't feel the pressure to contribute to the conversation because they don't care. Perfect.

"Can we go to your house?" she asked.

What are you doing? I don't know. I do know God made me this way and He "supposedly" doesn't make mistakes. *He also made pychopaths, but that doesn't give them the freedom to kill people, but don't think beyond yourself right now.*

We went my house since Mom was visiting family in Illinois for the week. I had the place to myself.

"Do you have anything to watch? I like porn," she said, staring holes through me with those blue eyes.

"I've got one. It's not very good though."

Laughing, "Are any of them 'good'?"

Took the tape out of the VCR, put in the video, pressed play. We fumbled over each other and this was the first time I wasn't physically hurt and crying afterward. I thought this must be right. She left afterward and I started thinking of a whole new world that I hadn't considered before, because God did say, "For you formed my inward parts; you knitted me together in my mother's womb. I praise you, for I am fearfully and wonderfully made..." (Psalm 139:13–14a). I remember that verse because it helped me when I got suicidal. It was effective here too.

God also said, "Or do you not know that the unrighteous will not inherit the kingdom of God? Do not be deceived: neither the sexually immoral, nor idolators, nor adulterers, nor men who practice homosexuality, nor thieves, nor the greedy, nor swindlers will inherit the kingdom of God" (1 Corinthians 6:9–10). But why would I want to read and believe the whole Bible? I'll just take what I like and dismiss the rest.

When Mom got home and tried to record *Star Trek* on the VCR, the tape started playing instead. She knocked on my bedroom door and handed the tape to me. "This is yours."

Oops.

Zoom Out

Spring 1999

I dropped out of college my second semester because I didn't want to write a story about the differences between a "black person" and "white person" in English. My creative writing professor was always sharing what I perceived as really stupid insights into the differences between said races. When he asked me to write this paper, as the only black person in class I told him that the difference was education and nothing more, but he didn't agree. I then retorted that since he was apparently blacker than me, he could write it himself.

Ticked off that an old white guy was going to tell me about my personal experiences with black folks, I left for greener pastures. I joined the military. For three years, I learned how to become a Light-Wheel Vehicle Mechanic, 63B. I worked on military vehicles whose weight was less than five tons and had wheels instead of tank tracks. Then came an honorable discharge and I went to truck-driving school.

I didn't dislike my time in the military, but I didn't exactly like it either. But driving? Driving I loved! The alone time, the not-being-babysat time, the choosing of my own schedule. The pickup time was 8 a.m. I got there and loaded by 10 a.m. (hopefully), and the rest of my day was mine as long as I was on my way from point A to point B. Customers didn't care how it got there, just that it got there. Perfect for someone who hates the idea of having some middle-management type justifying their job by bothering me.

Then I met a guy at a service plaza on the Indiana Toll Road. He seemed nice enough to hang out with while going down the road. We talked over our McDonald's lunches, and then over the CB going toward Harrisburg, PA. Then I did the dumbest thing I'd ever done in my life. In Harrisburg, I had sex with him in his truck. We did use protection, but as stated on the label, condoms are not 100% effective against pregnancy or the transmission of

STDs. Or so I found out for myself three weeks later, when the calm physician's assistant at the VA told me I was pregnant.

My heart sank. I didn't want this. I didn't have a home, a car; I'd been living in the truck since it was cheaper that way. What was I to do now? She looked at me and could tell this was not a planned parenthood, so she suggested what people there would've suggested: an abortion. *Hell no*, I thought, but said I needed time to digest this news. I had borrowed my mom's car to get to this appointment, so I needed to be going. I didn't want to talk to someone whose first option was killing. I had caused the actions that had led to this, but killing the baby wasn't a reasonable solution to this situation. Over the time it took to get to my mom's job and then get us both to her home, I decided on adoption. I knew I was not parent material, much less as a single parent. I was barely competent at taking care of myself.

I explained the situation to her, and she thought I was making the right choice. I did cry about it that night, but knew this was what had to be done. But what was I supposed to do about my job? I couldn't be driving all over the country when I needed to start prenatal care and such. So, I gave notice and quit. I found a local driving job through a temp service that had me driving a yard truck and just moving trailers around. Great people to work with and regular hours, but only one problem: getting in and out all day of a yard truck, the weirdly small trucks that pick up trailers by raising the fifth wheel. The door to get in and out is on the backside of the cab, in front of the trailer, and was eventually going to be impossible to navigate once my stomach got big enough.

I stayed there as long as I could, but one day it became physically too much for me, and I had to quit. Then I swallowed my pride and went on public assistance. I've never liked owing anyone anything, and public assistance was the ultimate at knowing I owed everyone everything. Sitting in the hot government building waiting for my number to be called, listening to the guy across from me have a very loud and animated conversation with someone only he could see, I swore I would never be in this situation again. I would not become someone dependent on the government for anything. Even as a veteran, I didn't want anything I didn't earn. Feeling at what I thought was my lowest point, I signed up for food stamps and rental assistance to help pay for a place to stay until I could give birth.

Then was the fight to keep myself alive. Battling depression my whole life, I thought I'd be okay for the time being, but that proved to be almost impossible. I'd spent two weeks in a mental health institution as a teenager, and I pretty much lied my way out of there. (I suspected they only released me because they thought if I'd put forth enough effort to lie about it, I must be alright.) I knew then, as I knew now, that I'd been lying to myself and not actually getting any help because I thought I knew what I was doing. I was a smoker because I knew both my mom and dad had died of cancer. So since cancer was a part of me, well, smoking was my way of passive-aggressively killing myself.

I found a cheap place and tried getting a part-time job to make ends meet, but the government told me I was making too much at the part-time gig, and that if I didn't quit they'd cancel my food stamps. Well, the assistance didn't come close to paying for anything, and the part-time job didn't either. *What should I do? Get fired and collect unemployment instead? Wait, part-timers don't get unemployment, idiot. That gas oven sure looks inviting. I should just end this charade now; get it over with. It would be best for everyone involved, right? Of course. But before you go, stop by the family cookout and have one last nice time with everyone before you check out.*

My cousins were off the chain, as usual—music, grilling, smack-talking, and just catching up on what everyone's been doing. I told a cousin about putting the baby up for adoption, and she told me one of my other cousins was trying to have a baby.

Wait, what? Really? She relayed the message to this cousin, and we spoke about my situation a week later. She said she'd be more than happy to adopt my child if that was truly what I wanted. I didn't want *any* of this, but here I was. So yeah, it was what I wanted, I guess.

An eight-pound, six-ounce, twenty-one-inch-long baby girl was born on November 22. She was beautiful. I didn't really know what I thought I expected, but she was more than that. I knew she deserved a better life than what I could provide, so I put her up for open familial adoption, and my cousin became her mother.

I got another over-the-road driving job, but I wouldn't be starting until after the first of the year. I asked and my cousin let me spend all of Christmas Day with my girl.

Zoom In
Winter 2000

Pittsburgh, PA, to St. Cloud, MN. I started driving that night at 6:30 p.m., looking forward to an easy night along the toll road. In Ohio, the speed limit, STRICTLY enforced, was 55 mph, and I'd gotten a ticket a couple of years ago for testing the "STRICTLY" part of that. Yeah, 57 in a 55 zone, $75 out the window. So, not wanting to give the state any more money, I was going the speed limit of 55 mph.

When I reached the merge of I-90, I started hearing people carrying on a rather vulgar conversation on the CB. I figured that it was a man and woman in each truck and, by their conversation, I was hoping they weren't related. Reasoning that they'd joined my westerly direction, I slowed down, hoping they would pull away from me, and I wouldn't have to hear their promises of oral satisfaction. Did I mention vulgar?

It took a long time for them to get far enough ahead of me not to hear what they were saying. In the meantime, I'd lowered the volume on the CB and was listening to the radio. Eventually I came across a construction zone that had traffic backed up, and I caught up to them again. And, yes, they were still being disgusting. Other drivers were now telling, asking, singing and screaming for the four of them to stop, but they were just getting worse and worse as time went on.

Of course, I could've just turned the CB off and been done with it, but now it was funny how angry the other drivers were getting. It was like reading a fight on social media—you can't scroll past that! Since I was upset, too, I lived vicariously through them.

The construction zone ended, and everyone took off in the Ohio 55-mph slow crawl race to Indiana. The vulgar voices slowly started to disappear again, so back to my music. No, wait, Ohio enjoys construction zones so much, let's do one again! And again…and again. *Hey, now the toll road is three lanes all the way across, and the speed limit is 70 mph. Be happy.* But you guessed it. Every time we slowed down, The Vulgars would be on the CB.

This happened all the way to Indiana, and at the toll booth we were all back, bunched up again. The difference this time was that now we were going into a state with a less "STRICTLY" enforced speed limit. After what seemed like a lifetime of listening to grossness, and cursing to make the grossness stop, I grabbed the toll ticket and put my entire foot on the accelerator to get away. So did everyone else.

It was about 11:30 p.m. when I heard a voice on the CB call me by my company name. "[Tonia's Company], what's the speed limit on this road?"

If you paid me money, I'd have said that the voice I heard was one of the guys I'd been listening to all night, so I answered accordingly, "You drive your truck, nasty f*cker, and I'll drive mine."

Then I noticed something I hadn't heard in almost four hours: silence. No one was talking on the CB. I looked in the mirror, and a vehicle was catching up to me rather quickly. *Uh-oh.* He started flashing the red and blue lights as he got right next to me, and before I could think, he turned them off. "What's the speed limit?" I heard again on the CB.

"60." I turned the CB off and drove 60 mph.

Zoom Out
2001

Until I got pregnant, I used to believe my poop didn't stink, and that I could do whatever I wanted and skate by without much, if any consequences. But after the baby, life was a different story. I was so depressed—maybe postpartum, maybe my own naturally depressed state of mind just a little juiced up—but whatever it was, it was keeping me down. I'd fantasize about driving into bridge supports. I'd pray for God not to wake me up when I went to sleep. It was bad.

Then I met a guy who worked at the same trucking company as I did, and we became friends. Our mutual friend "let it slip" that he was interested in me, and I of course thought that was cool. We talked often and decided it would be good for us to move in together on our way to having a "relationship." I didn't know what I was doing; hadn't really dated anyone in high school, or college, or the military. So sure, what could go wrong? Hey, I know! Let's get married, too!

Before we got married, I moved into his house. He lived in Nebraska, and since my address in Michigan was more for mail purposes than anything else, the move was easy. He gave me a key right before he went back out on the road, but the first time I went to the house it didn't work. I called him and he said, "Climb in a window." Okay, pause. I wear my hair very short, like a guy. I tend to wear clothing a bit too big but not baggy. The house was in a predominantly white neighborhood, where no one knew me, and it was late at night. I hadn't yet lived at this house long enough to have gotten any mail delivered, so there was no proof I was supposed to be here. *Climb in a window? Umm, no.*

We worked out the key situation, and I moved in the next time I was in town. It was weird for me to think of myself as not living in Michigan anymore. I was learning about a new city: where the grocery store was, the bank, the closest place to buy smokes, etc. But we fell into a routine, and I realized I had made a huge mistake marrying this man. I kept my feelings to myself and just seemed to get swept up in what I wanted, thinking I could "fake it 'til I make it," since that's what they tell you in therapy about getting through the tough times.

Driving across the country was what was keeping me sane. I was depressed, and I had my moments of despair, but I kept the wheels rolling and tried to get my head right. I happened to be in Indiana when I was down and hurting. What's the deal with Indiana and heartbreak? I missed my daughter even though I didn't know her. I wanted to see her but knew I couldn't. I stopped at a rest area to park for the night, and I started crying. I closed the curtains on the truck cab and sat on the bed with the only picture I had of her. My girl was two years old now. I hoped she was well. I vowed to kill my cousin if anything bad happened to her. I just hurt so bad.

"I WILL GIVE YOU MORE."

The words were suddenly coming from everywhere and nowhere. I felt them vibrate through my bones and echo in my head. I was terrified and calm, filled with fear yet knowing I was safe. How does one describe hearing the voice of God? I know you probably think I'm nuts, but I completely understand now when the Israelites asked God to speak to Moses instead of directly to them (Exodus 20:19). The Scriptures say His voice is like a whisper (1 Kings 19:12b), but no part of that was a whisper! It was loud and clear!

I laid facedown in the bunk of that truck and cried like I'd never cried before. I worshipped Him in that moment. I didn't want to be a parent, never had, but Him saying "I will give you more" meant I wouldn't have to feel like this, that the "more" would be different and better the next time. As the Scriptures say, "…it was credited to him as righteousness" (Genesis 15:6). Abraham didn't know how God was going to pull it off, but he believed Him, so I would too. However God wanted to do things, I was game. I just didn't want to be so depressed.

Then stepped in a blessing. She was our next-door neighbor. We started speaking occasionally to each other—you know, the casual "hi-bye" friendly wave and small talk. In the winter I'd shovel her driveway; in the summer I'd cut her grass. Our love of the macabre brought us together, watching *Investigation Discovery* for hours on end, laughing at the dumb things people would do to each other and/or thought they could get away with. (The detective said, "It's either a stranger, a family member or a friend." We looked at each other and simultaneously asked, laughing uproariously, "Who doesn't fall into one of those categories?")

Our friendship grew immensely. Then she got pregnant. I don't mean to sound ominous, but when she had a baby girl, I was right there. Not knowing if this was what God meant in His message to me, but assuming it had something to do with it, I became "Auntie Tonia." That little girl meant the world to me. Being in school and working at a warehouse now, I was on a regular schedule and home. I was the babysitter. I was the one teaching her how to get in trouble like a good aunt should. But things weren't meant to stay that way. She and her mom moved to be closer to relatives in Colorado, so I was left in a marriage I didn't want and with no other friends.

Acquiring Satelites... 11%
March 2005

My husband had a car that needed new tires, a new battery, and some other minor work done to it. He kept it in the garage, and I was particularly depressed since my best friend had moved to Colorado. I tried to slit my wrists but couldn't do it. So, I decided to sit in the car in the garage and die that way.

The car didn't have enough gas to run very long, and I had to jump-start it. Using the one-gallon gas can that was for the lawnmower, I put fuel in the car. It took a while to refill the tank, going back and forth to the gas station and getting one gallon at a time. Not to mention, it was my luck that the station was currently out of the larger gas cans.

When I thought I had enough gas in the car for it to run long enough for me to die, I put some towels along the bottom of the garage door, so all I had to do was close the door and sit in the car. But it wouldn't start. I took that car from a little under a quarter of a tank to over three-fourths, one gallon at a time, going back and forth for about three hours, and now it wouldn't start! *ARE YOU F*CKING SERIOUS!?!*

Acquiring Satellites...17%
Summer 2005

I found a way to blow up my marriage and hurt a man who didn't deserve the crap I put him through, for which I will be forever sorry. I went back to school and dropped out again, this time from ITT Tech, then wandered from company to company, getting fired multiple times. I learned a lot about myself in the meantime. Got evicted from a mobile home and got two cars repossessed.

Zoom In
May 2007

Passion was a good dog. She was a Great Dane mix I bought from some people outside a Tennessee Walmart. On the way home, I found out she had intestinal worms, lots of them, and they were pretty big. *Oh, the things you put up with when you love a pet, right?*

She eventually got healed and vaccinated, and we were off and running, me and my truck dog. Getting something to eat at a truck stop in Indiana (*oh, this state…*), a guy gave Passion a piece of hot dog. I don't like it when people feed my dog. She's got two jobs in the truck: my companion and my early threat detection system. Men who befriend my dog are not welcome. But before I could stop her, she had it down her big mouth. I smiled and pulled her away, with him looking at me like I'm a b*tch.

After about ten minutes, going toward Indianapolis, she started hacking—violently. I pulled over and let her out. Vomit and diarrhea. Poor thing. I got her back in the truck and she laid on the bed, asleep in no time flat. I checked on her again when I stopped to get fuel just south of the city. She wasn't breathing! No! I looked up the nearest emergency veterinarian and headed that way. I dropped the trailer at the truckstop and got her to the doc. I knew she was already dead but what else could I do? The doc said he would have her cremated. I never returned to pick up the ashes.

It's now been a month without Passion. My brother is cleaning out his deep freeze and cooking some stuff. All us siblings have been invited to come eat. I've finished my food and am the only one at the party without a plate, when a little black and tan mutt of a dog comes over and sits at my feet. "Whose dog?" I ask.

"It's the neighbor's. They've been moving out and they leave the dog tied up to that pole over there." He points to a clothesline pole in their backyard. "I haven't seen the people in a couple days, and I don't think they're coming back. I went over this morning and let the dog go but it hasn't left the trailer park. Animal control has been through here twice but ain't caught it yet!"

Wondering why this dog has come to the one person without food, it feels providential. While debating whether I'm ready for another dog, we see the animal control truck come up the street.

"Come on, dog," I say, race-walking to my car and opening the door. Dog jumps right in, like that was the plan from the beginning. I take her home and name her Shai.

Zoom In

Spring 2008

Dallas, TX, to Charlottesville, VA. Dark. Fog so thick you couldn't see the mirrors on the end of the hood. *Why am I even out here tonight?* This was nuts. White-knuckling the wheel and barely going 25 mph. Getting close to Memphis, TN, but at this speed it'd take a year or two. It's moments like these when I laugh at those who love speed. When driving a vehicle weighing in around 80,000 pounds, speed is not your friend. It's not how fast you can go; it's how fast you can stop!

Some people had decided to park on the shoulder because they couldn't see. *Guess what? You're not completely on the shoulder, and it would be nice if you could turn on your four-way flashers too. I don't know why you're parking, though. It's not like the fog is going away anytime soon.*

CRAP! Trucks trying to merge onto the interstate. Turn signals on and everything! I couldn't see jack! *Maybe I should park on the shoulder too.*

"Hey, Bo, where ya at?" The voice from the CB was faint but getting louder.

"Imma comin'. Whatcha pegged at?"

"I slowed down to 60 for ya. Now, let's get across here!"

60! Are you two nuts? There is no way! I'm making diamonds in my underwear, and they're going 60 mph?

"I'm at 70. I'll be right there."

I could see some taillights in front of me. I was catching up to this truck pretty quickly. I thought I was going a little too fast at 25 mph, but maybe the fog would clear up in a few miles. I'd sit here for a minute or two and let the two speed demons pass me before I tried getting around this truck. I knew Bo would not be able to stop in time if I got in the left lane.

I gave it a few minutes, but I was too impatient. Maybe Bo and his friend were going the other direction, and I was waiting like a moron. *Take a deep breath, and here we go.*

I got out in the passing lane and stepped on it. That's right— 30 mph and steadily climbing. Passing the truck, I looked over, and he had red dashboard lights all over. Thinking *that's got to get annoying after a while,* I saw him key up his CB.

"I think I sees ya lights. Flash 'em so I know that's you." The truck in front of him flashed his trailer lights. "Yep, I'll back her down now. A nice and easy 65 should be good for now, right?"

"It took your slow *ss long enough to get up here."

I laughed.

Zoom Out
Summer 2012

I met her on one of those online dating apps. We talked a lot at first and she seemed to get my level of craziness like I thought I got hers.

We'd met up a couple of times and I introduced her to my friends and family. She had me do the same. I even stayed with her when I took my home-time from work. My dog met her dog and we all seemed to be getting along when things just changed.

I'd like to say I knew exactly when it happened, but I don't. I remember a phone call when I was really tired and she hung up on me because she said, "You don't love me anymore! You probably have a girlfriend somewhere else!"

First, I know I haven't told you I loved you yet, and second, I'm too indifferent to juggle multiple relationships. I tried to call her back and talk but she wouldn't answer the phone. So, I went to sleep.

I didn't really like the feelings I had with her, but I didn't like them with my ex-husband either. I thought I knew what love was, but I'd recently started to wonder if I did. I had no interest in working hard to build a relationship; if it didn't just fall into place, then it wasn't going to work anyway, right?

But then she pushed it way too far. She tried to get rid of my dog.

Shai had a huge lump growing on the side of her head. I took her to the vet, and she was diagnosed with cancer. Doc told me she might live two to three more years. They performed the lumpectomy and put her head in a protective cone to heal. I didn't want her uncomfortable in the truck with that cone, so girlfriend and I agreed for her to stay home for the two weeks of healing.

Then I missed a text message, or I didn't reply fast enough, I forget which. By the time I looked at the phone, girlfriend texted, "I'm taking your dog to the pound and leaving her since you aren't talking to me!"

Oh, hell no!

I explained that the state of Wyoming doesn't have great cell phone coverage, but she wasn't responding anymore. That was it. I got a load going back to her place; I used my key to get in; I got my dog, my clothes, and anything else I'd put in her place; and I left.

I felt so relieved when Shai and I were on the road again. Somewhere along the way I realized that my relief wasn't just about having my dog safe, but that it had felt weird to me to be with a woman. I don't know how to explain it. Like it was forced. I knew how I felt around men: don't trust any to love me or care for me, since they would all hurt me eventually. But being with a woman just wasn't good either.

I got to one of my company's terminals, made sure Shai was okay, then went to a bar. The shuttle that went from the terminal to Walmart, to the motel, then to "restaurant row" dropped me off at a bar, and I bellied up. I had a blast pretending I was fine. Pretending that I wasn't angry at God for making me go through what I'd went through when I was younger. Pretending it didn't bother me losing a crazy relationship that was going nowhere fast. Making me not trust anyone. Trust your parents, they die. Trust your family, they abuse you. Trust your instincts, they lead you down a path that makes you feel dirty. *Thanks God, You're just great!*

I stayed so late that the shuttle ended its service, and I had to walk back to the yard. That was fine; maybe I'd get hit by a truck and it would all be over.

Staggered all the way to the truck. Got in and was asleep before my head hit the pillow. Shai woke me up some time later and I moved the truck 100 feet to be closer to the grass to let her out. Security guard saw that and told the company. In the morning, I was fired for operating a commercial vehicle while intoxicated.

God, why can't You do anything FOR me?!

Zoom Out
Summer 2018

Shai's cancer took over. When she'd gotten so bad that I had to carry her outside to do her business, I knew she didn't have long. I couldn't bring myself to put her down at the vet, and as I watched her refuse to eat and barely sleep, I chided myself for my weakness. On June 24, the day before my birthday, my dog lay down and never woke up again.

The loss of my dog was hard on me. My job had been scaling back on hours, and bills were starting to mount up. I'd sold my car in May in an effort to stay afloat, and rode my motorcycle back and forth to work since it was paid for. Nope, some kind of fuel injector problem with the bike, and now I was spending most of my paycheck on ride services (public transportation didn't run when I needed to go to work). Desperate to keep my job, I signed on the dotted line for an overpriced piece of crap that was almost as expensive as my rent. I couldn't keep up the payments, rent, credit cards, utilities, etc. This was futile.

Street View:

She always says, "If you need anything, let me know," so I'll see how far that really goes. I asked for money to help pay my rent and she came over. She sat with me and helped me work out a budget and listened as I cried, trying to explain the situation. She hugged me and we watched a comedy show that made me feel better. I wasn't quite sure how I'd pay her back, but I had a little breathing room.

I struggled to eke out an existence for a while. Robbing Peter to pay Paul, as they say, but not getting anywhere. Hopelessness was my breakfast, lunch and dinner. Depression makes a person feel lost, like there's not going to be anything worthwhile tomorrow. No job, no one loves you, it's only going to be this misery forever. In the short-sidedness of that thinking, I chose to end it this time. I got my gun and held it to my head and, through tears and anguish that seemed to never leave, I pulled the trigger. It didn't fire. *Was the safety on?* I checked—*no*. I pointed at a pillow on the couch and pulled the trigger. *BANG!* I paced around the room for a minute, then sat back down, held it up, and *CLICK!*

I doubled over in emotional pain. "Why won't You leave me alone and let this happen?" I yelled at Him. I got no response. Balled up on the floor, afraid to try a third time, I just laid there and cried. At some point I got up, got in the car, and drove to the emergency room, where I was admitted.

I stayed there for two weeks, getting my medications adjusted and signing up for therapy. Afterward, I did outpatient therapy for about six weeks. I still felt the same. This was my life. I would just never know happiness. "Fake it 'til you make it," huh? I'd been "faking it," so I resigned myself to the idea that living out this misery was "making it."

Zoom In
May 2019

I'd delivered to two stores. On my way back to the yard to reload the trailer. *That gives rush-hour time to go away, and I'll be able to get in and out of the last three stores relatively easily. Then back to the yard, load up, park and done,* I thought.

"Why are you back already?" the foreman asked.

"I'm going to do the last three stores after I reload." Getting my scale ticket off the printer.

He got up and walked toward me in that I'm-mad-at-you way he does. "I needed you to do it the way it was planned!" Pointing his fingers in my face like I was a bad child.

Backing up, I said, "I always do it this way and you know it." Swiping his hand out of my face.

"That's it! Go!" Pointing out toward the truck.

"Hey! What's going on in here?" The plant manager came out of his office in response to the yelling. I listened almost quietly as the foreman poorly explained what he saw as me hitting him.

"I did not hit him!" I stated. "He came running over here pointing his fingers in my face and I swatted them away!"

"Tonia, gotta go now," manager said. "I'll watch the tape."

I stepped outside. The foreman had never stepped to me like that before, but I'd seen him talk to other drivers like children. I guess I should've known he'd do it with me eventually.

I got the truck loaded and parked. I went inside to get the paperwork for the last three stores. "Come in here." Manager waved me into his office.

"You watched that, right?" I asked.

"Yes." He sat behind his desk and handed me a write-up form. "You made contact with him, and I have no wiggle room. I've got to suspend you."

"What?! Seriously?"

"The video will be reviewed at headquarters, but as of right now, I have to suspend you for a week."

I snatched up the paper and signed. "Do I have to finish today?"

"No."

I stood up and walked out of the building. They fired me over the phone at the end of the week.

Zoom Out

Spring 2020

I started reading the Bible every day. I didn't know where to start, so I started at the beginning: Genesis 1:1. I didn't do what I'd done in the past as far as just reading it as a novel, but instead I researched what I was reading. I got a commentary and a biblical reference book and also started listening to modern authors and their commentaries. I completely got rid of all my secular music, including my favorite, Janet Jackson. I bought all new Christian music: MercyMe, Casting Crowns, Kirk Franklin, Bizzle, Jordan Feliz, Lecrae, NF, Skillet, For Today, Phinehas, etc. I stopped listening to the news and deleted all except one of my social media accounts.

Recalculating...85%

I used to want to watch the rapists in my past explain before God why they did what they did. I'm sure I wasn't the first or the last of their victims, so when God would pretend to listen to the bullsh*t they'd say, then give them the ultimate smackdown from Heaven, I wanted to be there. To be a fly on the wall of their beginning torment in eternal Hell. But I don't want that anymore. To know Jesus is to know love; hope; peace. To know that I may not be a rapist, but I deserve that sentence to Hell, too. God doesn't have first-, second- or third-degree sin; it's all punishable by death in comparison to Him. We are all the sinner condemned to death, saved by His grace like Jesus Barabbas (Matthew 27:21). We don't deserve His mercy, but He chooses us. Like Him, I should do what God wants for me, not my own evil vengeance. I want to see those who have hurt me in the past in Heaven in the future. Forgive and love your enemy like God has forgiven you (Matthew 6:14–15, Romans 12:17). What an awesome place Heaven will be.

I started attending church online every Sunday. I joined some small groups and met some new people. I started paying tithes to the church and learning how to pray. I also started serving the church online as a chatroom host. It was the only way I could help out even though I wasn't physically there, so it was perfect. I never understood what Paul meant when he'd talk about the mysteries of God until I started to learn who God is. When I'd hold on to things so tightly that I couldn't live without them, I would become devastated when I lost them. When I thought I was in control of my money, I was spending it on things I didn't need, racking up debt. When I started giving Him His money, I spent it more wisely, getting out of debt and obtaining a raise, in essence. When I stopped thinking of the things I had as being mine, I started taking better care of them. My job isn't mine. It's where God has placed me for the time being. The company could go bankrupt, or the owners could simply decide they don't want to do it anymore. But God will put me in the next position He wants me in.

I also had to do some forgiving of family members who didn't know what was in my head. They did their best with the information they had, but I'm not now, nor was I then, the type to let anyone know how I was feeling. That first learned lesson of Don't-Tell-Anyone became Don't-Tell-Anyone-Anything.

My foster mom was the only person who believed in me in those early years and hasn't lost that belief. Observing her just being herself, taught me that God's plans aren't like making wishes. That God doesn't make "only" people. "I'm only a truck driver." When God made me, He made me much more that an "only" person. I'm "fearfully and wonderfully made (Psalm 139:1)" "in His image (Genesis 1:26)" and "only" is a starting point, not the finish line (Romans 5:4–5).

Recalculating... 89%
Zoom In

I wonder what it'll be like to be "caught up" (1 Thessalonians 4:17) into Heaven. Will it be like flying through the air, being able to feel the wind on your body, being able to see the world getting smaller behind you? Or will it be like a blink—one minute you're here and the next you're there? Closing my eyes, I am immediately surrounded by whiteness like fog. I get the sensation of looking around, trying to get my bearings, but I can't see anything. The feeling of love is overwhelming, though. An unconditional love. The love you pretend to attribute to pets, but this is more! Every evil I've ever done is known here, but I'm still loved. Every mistake I've made is known here, but I'm still loved.

Opening my eyes, I'm in the bunk of the truck and all of a second has passed in time, but I know I just touched Heaven. Thank you, Lord.

Zoom Out
Winter 2020

I got the idea of leasing my own truck. As a lease/purchase owner-operator, I thought I'd get more options available to me, such as getting to choose the cities and states where I would pick up and deliver. However, I'm responsible for everything with the truck, such as fuel, insurance and maintenance issues. I'd be leasing a truck from a rental company because I didn't have the credit to buy one from a dealership. It would probably have been an older truck anyway, maybe a model from 2016 or older with half a million miles on it. I was dreaming of paying that truck off in a few years and being able to buy a new truck as my next truck. The paint job was going to be awesome!

I started praying to see if God would be favorable to this idea. I tried to make a deal with Him, so I gave myself a goal to accomplish in order even to ask Him: save $10,000. I was almost there when I started to plan this, but I still needed about $4,000.

I reached the financial goal and then started putting in applications. These days, it's just one application posted to many trucking recruiters' websites, but my app was out there. And yes, here came the onslaught of companies wanting company drivers, who I had to tell I was looking to be an owner-operator. After I got all of those out of the way, I narrowed it down to three potential places I wanted to work because their trucks were newer, which meant fewer maintenance issues (hopefully) and an amount of freight to keep me moving and paying the bills. Two of the companies were primarily owner-operator-based, meaning most of their drivers were owners. The last was a very large company with dedicated routes in the southeast if I didn't like being over-the-road anymore.

My first rejection came from one of the owner-operator companies. They sent an email stating that they couldn't hire me because I had been fired from a previous employer. Okay, one down, two to go, right? The second rejection came after the large company just stopped talking to me. I couldn't get any of them on the phone or even to reply to an email about the status of my application.

The third rejection was the hardest. This was the company I actually wanted to be a driver for. I spoke to the recruiter almost every day for about three weeks. He kept getting pushback from my previous employers about when I had worked there and why I didn't work there anymore. I finally had to intervene and ask for the information myself, to which they replied that the recruiter wasn't sending in the proper paperwork for them to release the info. So I ended up being my own recruiter, trying to get hired at a company that already had recruiters!

Now, this entire time I'd been praying daily about all things, but this especially. I was constantly asking God not to let me go where He didn't send me, not to let me stray too far from His path for me, and I was badgering Him in the spirit of the Parable of the Persistent Widow (Luke 18:1–8). If He didn't want this, I didn't want this either. During my normal Bible study, a few verses popped up. Psalms 37:4 states, "Take delight in the Lord, and he will give you the desires of your heart." I definitely desired this, and I did take delight in the Lord. Could He be telling me it was a go? 1 Corinthians 7:21 says, "Were you a slave when you were called? Don't let it trouble you—although if you can gain your freedom, do so." Not saying that working as a company driver is anything close to slavery, but the thought of the added freedom of owning my own business was something to pursue. And, of course, there's Colossians 3:23: "Whatever you do, work at it with all your heart, as working for the Lord, not for human masters." Can you even have anything work-related without sticking this verse in the mix? I took all those verses and more and told myself, "Yep, He's on my side!"

The company finally got the needed paperwork, and scheduled a place for me to pick up the rental car and drive to orientation to start this new path! I put in my notice with my current employer, and they said they didn't want me to go and even sent me a packet about being an owner-operator with them. I would've done it if I could've financed my own, but as I said before, my credit was shot.

A week before I was going to start this new ride, the company called and said they couldn't hire me because they hadn't noticed the firing in my work history. The deal was off. My old company had never wanted me to leave, so I was hoping they would take me back, although there was no guarantee about that. I let them know I was no longer leaving, and three people sent me text messages thanking me for staying. *Wow, didn't expect that!* During this whole adventure, I kept getting loads assigned to specific places I'd asked for. I got time off just because I asked. I got paid to sit with a load for five days after a winter storm went through the South, where no one knows how to drive in the snow, so my receiver closed and my appointment was rescheduled for five days later. I was even Driver of the Month! I could pretty much go where I wanted when I wanted…Wait, wasn't that what I was looking for as an owner-operator? So, what I hear myself saying is, I have no responsibility for fuel costs, insurance premiums, maintenance issues, health insurance, worker's comp, etc., BUT I go where I want, do what I want, when I want…? What exactly am I a slave to again?

But let's not stop there! When that call came telling me they weren't going to hire me, I was heartbroken. I thought God had paved the way for me. All those dreams of the kind of paint job I'd have on the truck, declaring my love of the Lord God Almighty! *What do You mean, "No?"* Then stepped in the story of King David and the building of the Temple. In 2 Samuel 7:1-17, King David asks God's prophet, Nathan, if he should build a temple to God, and Nathan tells him that (I'm paraphrasing a little) God loves whatever you do, so why not? Go for it. But God stops things before they can get started and tells David that he is not the one who will ultimately build the Temple to The Most High, but that it will be one of his offspring. The important part, for me, was when I realized that David had set his hopes on doing this to glorify the Lord, and the Lord told him, "No." How must that have felt?

But what did David do? 2 Samuel 7:18 tells us: "Then King David went in and sat before the LORD and said, "Who am I, O Lord GOD, and what is my house, that you have brought me thus far?" Not trying to be melodramatic here, but I had to readjust my heartbreak. Who am I to feel like I deserved something? That God had let me down or tricked me? Didn't I ask for freedom in my job? Didn't I ask for being able to pick and choose? Didn't I ask for Him to keep me from going too far from His path for me? He didn't let me drive to the place and only THEN find out I wasn't hired. I still had my job. So, what are you missing? Nothing, oh Lord, forgive me in my arrogance.

Nope, wait, I was still missing a new truck. Well, my company told me they were moving me into 2022 trucks. After all of this, He was still blessing me despite my sinful nature, not because of anything I did but because He is a merciful, loving and long-suffering God (Psalms 78:38, 86:15). I give Him all the praise!

Zoom In

Now

It seems as I look back at my choices, I made some good ones and some bad ones. I completely lost the road at times and had to find my way back with that little red truck on the screen, getting closer and closer to the lavender line. Trying to navigate without knowing how to read a GPS unit can be taxing. The red line doesn't mean you get to drive faster at that section of road; it means no one gets to drive faster than 10 mph there. Gray lines mean that it's pretty much a dirt road, and it isn't recommended for heavy vehicles unless you physically watch someone else drive down that road first.

One of the books that got me off my butt and into action is titled *Bearing God's Name* by Carmen Joy Imes. It taught me taking the Lord's name in vain isn't about swearing. It's about calling yourself a Christian but not living like one. We are called out to demonstrate God's love in this world as best we can. How can God show you His glory, His power, His work in your life if you refuse to attempt anything above your own ability?

I can only call my disregard of God's signs as plain stupid. Yeah, it's taken me a minute to pay attention, but now that I'm here, I can't ignore Him anymore. Hebrews 2:1 says, "Therefore we must pay much closer attention to what we have heard, lest we drift away from it." I heard God's words, I felt God's actions, and I drifted. No more.

When I started doing what I believed, I got out of debt, stopped doing things that would get me fired, and took responsibility, because I'm the one who will have to stand before Him and make an account (Hebrews 4:13, Revelation 20:15). I had to push myself into a new perspective: God Loves Me. It's no longer "fake it 'til you make it." It's "He knows. let Him love you anyway."

I started smoking when I was eleven. I tried quitting when I joined the military. All throughout basic training and Advanced Individual Training, I wasn't allowed to smoke. The second I graduated, I bought a pack of cigarettes, like I hadn't stopped smoking for those six months. I tried to quit when my niece was born. I managed to quit for over a year, but I went back when I got stressed. All the other times I'd tried, I kept wanting to smoke, knowing it was bad for me but unable to quit.

Last year, I asked God. Now, not only am I not smoking, I don't even want to, and that's the part that's different from all the times before. I don't want to die. I don't want to kill myself at all. The depression I've had my whole life; gone. What makes all this happen is putting my trust in Him.

Do you know what joy is? I thought I did until I actually did. I was studying the Bible like I wanted to know the truth. I confessed my sins to God and repented of promises I had no business making. I broke bonds of spiritual slavery, from smoking (slowly committing suicide) to dyslexia (I work hard to read His word) to homosexuality (that's not who He made me). I strive to be who He says I am and not who this world wants me to be.

God, be with me as I hang out with my friends. Let me show Your light in my life while I'm there. You said to "…be strong and courageous. To not be afraid because You'll be with me wherever I go" (Joshua 1:9). Don't let me shame You.

If You could let me know if I'm doing right, I'd like that. I need help making sure I'm following Your will. You know, I'm still new to this, Lord. Please, show me. In Jesus' name, I pray. Amen.

Acquiring Satellites…100%

"Happy birthday!" The best friend who sat with me on one of those suicidal nights hands me a little box wrapped with a ribbon. Jewelry? She knows I don't do jewelry. "I've been meaning to get you this for a good minute now. Hope you like it!"

As I pull off the ribbon and open the box, I see it's a gold crucifix I can wear on my necklace.

What's the feeling you get when you know, finally, that you're on the right road?

Joy.

How did I know I was so far from the route I needed that I had to backtrack? A perfectly working gun that didn't fire. A car that worked well enough suddenly wouldn't start. How did I know I was on the right road? I met my girl when she was 16. She now has two children of her own—a beautiful young family. I'm still Auntie and have gained another niece along the way.

It's not always easy to make that turn in the fog of uncertainty, and trust in someone greater than yourself. As you learn to trust in God's positioning system, you stop white-knuckling the wheel and squinting so hard out the windshield. Learning His word is how you learn to navigate.

Should I hide the cutting scars on my arms and be ashamed of myself? Psalms 103:12 says, "As far as the east is from the west, so far does he remove our transgressions from us." Should I walk around this truck-stop parking lot and pray over the drivers? James 5:16b states, "The prayer of the righteous is powerful and effective." Should I even bother writing all this out? I'm pretty sure no one wants to hear my sob story. But 1 Peter 4:10 NIV declares, "Each of you should use whatever gift you have received to serve others, as faithful stewards of God's grace in its various forms."

How are you following God's positioning system?

All Bible quotes from this story are from the English Standard Version

www.ingramcontent.com/pod-product-compliance
Lightning Source LLC
LaVergne TN
LVHW042003060526
838200LV00041B/1852